# Daddy's Blue Eyes

Written by

## Marnie L. Hill

Ilustrations by Sasha Baines

Victoria, BC, Canada
FriesenPress

**FriesenPress**

Suite 300 - 990 Fort St
Victoria, BC, V8V 3K2
Canada

www.friesenpress.com

**Copyright © 2018 by Marnie Hill**
First Edition — 2018

Illustrator: Sasha Baines

All rights reserved.

No part of this publication may be reproduced in any form, or by any means, electronic or mechanical, including photocopying, recording, or any information browsing, storage, or retrieval system, without permission in writing from FriesenPress.

ISBN
978-1-5255-2528-5 (Hardcover)
978-1-5255-2529-2 (Paperback)
978-1-5255-2530-8 (eBook)

*1. Family & Relationships, Death, Grief, Bereavement*

Distributed to the trade by The Ingram Book Company

## Dedicated

To Detective Constable Matthew Leslie and all who loved him. Matt died December 24, 1997 after a valiant fight with cancer.

His legacy lives on through the stories told and memories shared by his many friends, colleagues and family. Through his strength, courage, sense of humour and love of life, Matt inspired us all.

His death serves not to remind us of what we lost, but what we gained by being a part of his life.

My daddy is in heaven. He died when I was two years old and my sister was four. Daddy was a police officer. He liked to help people. But most of all he liked to keep children safe.

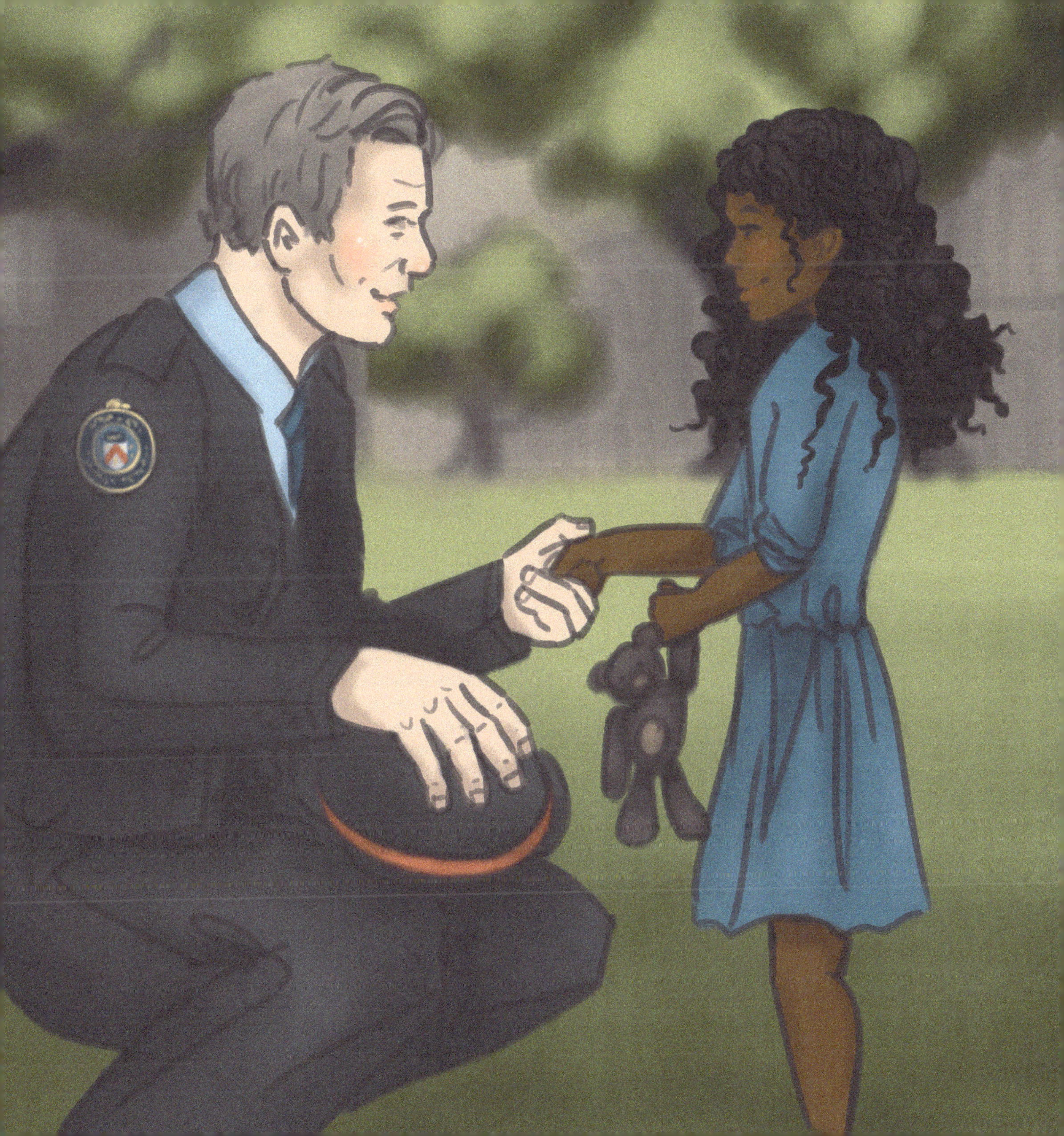

Once, Daddy and his police officer friends rode their bikes across Canada to raise money to help a little boy who was sick. The boy's family needed the money to buy medicine to help make him better.

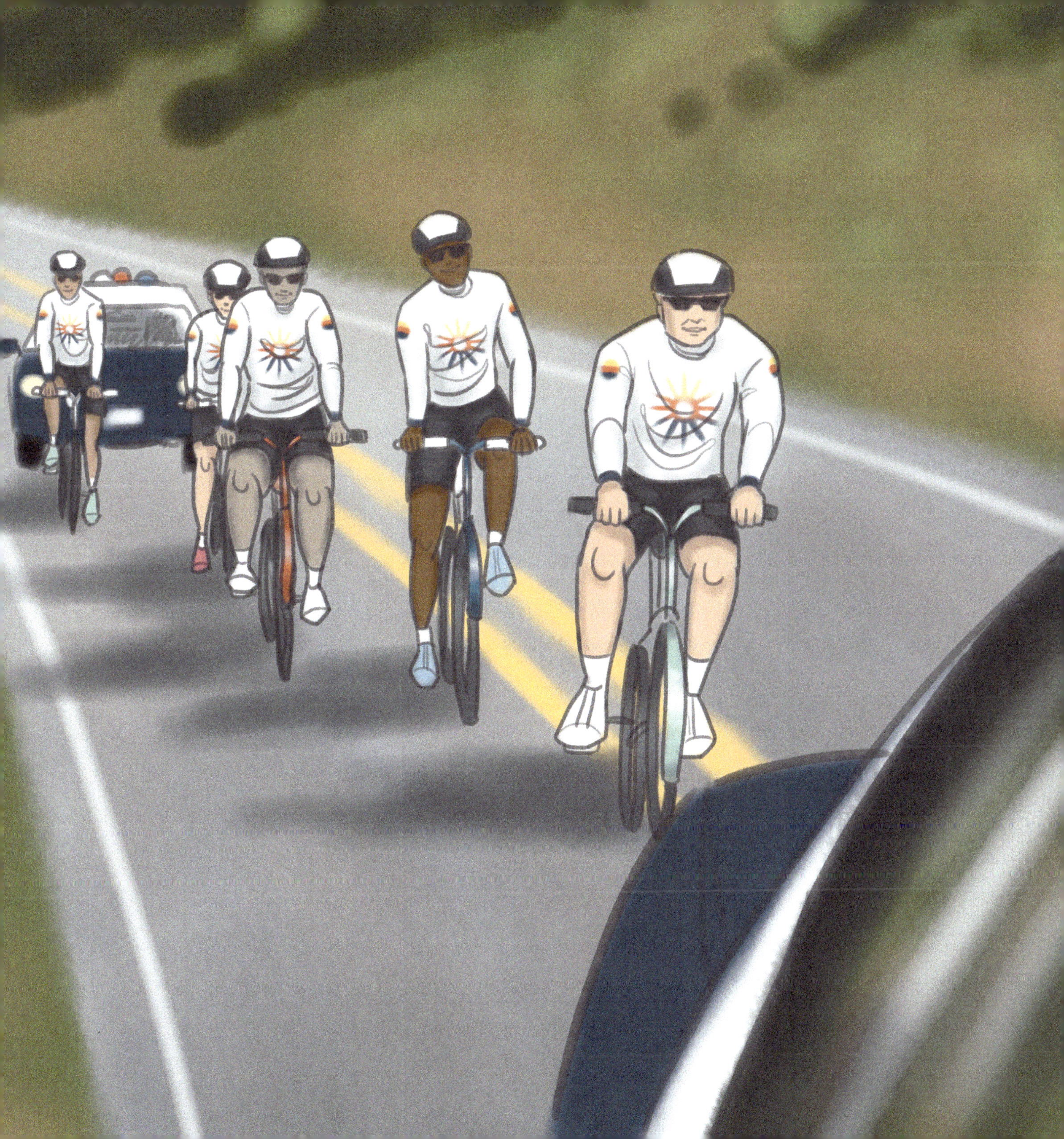

When Daddy wasn't working, he liked to play hockey, and he also liked to watch it on TV. In the summer, Daddy liked to ride his motorcycle. In the winter, he liked to ski.

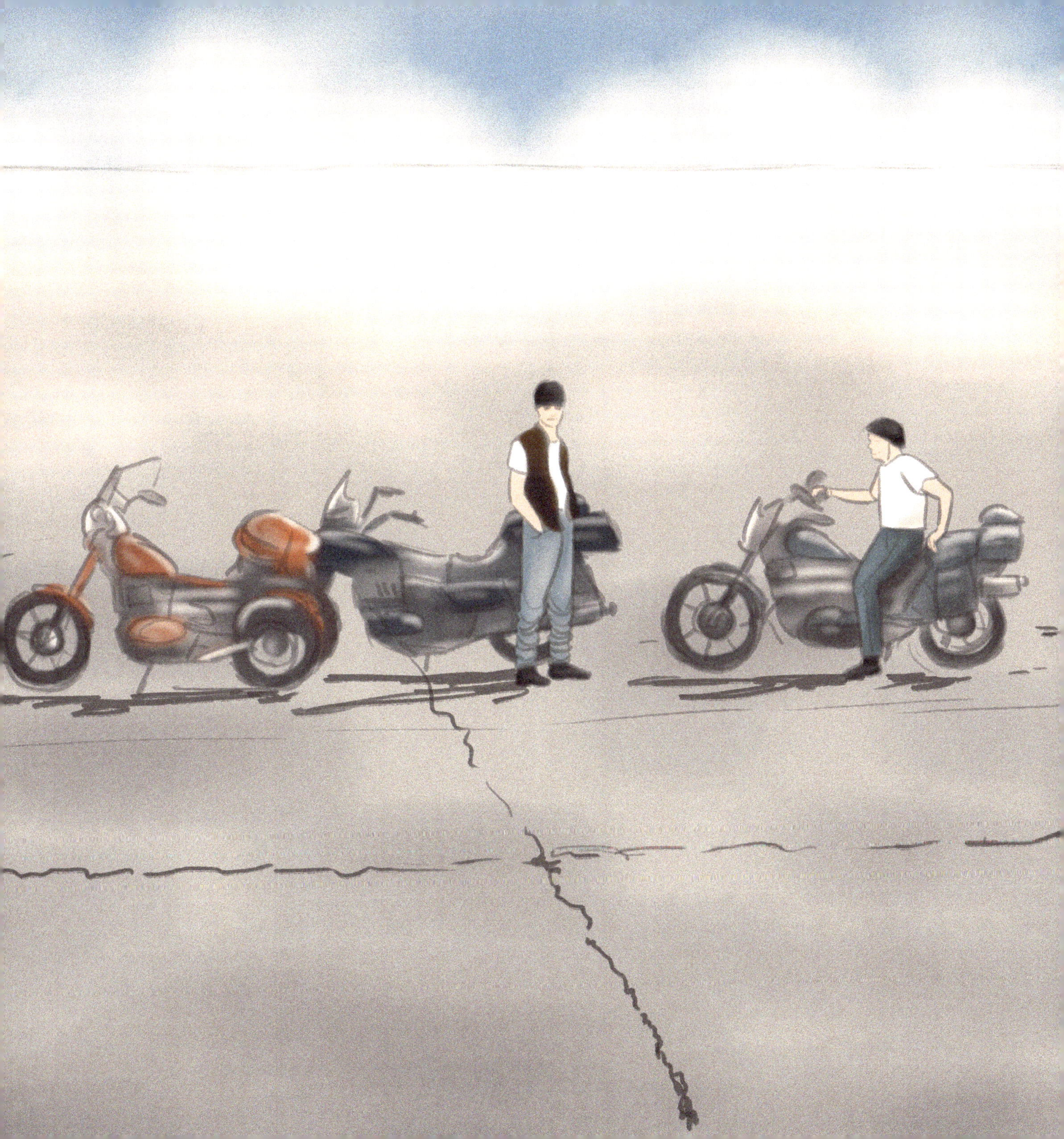

Daddy liked to do lots of things, but most of all he liked to spend time with my sister, my mommy and me. He would take us for long walks and push us high on the swings in the schoolyard behind our house.

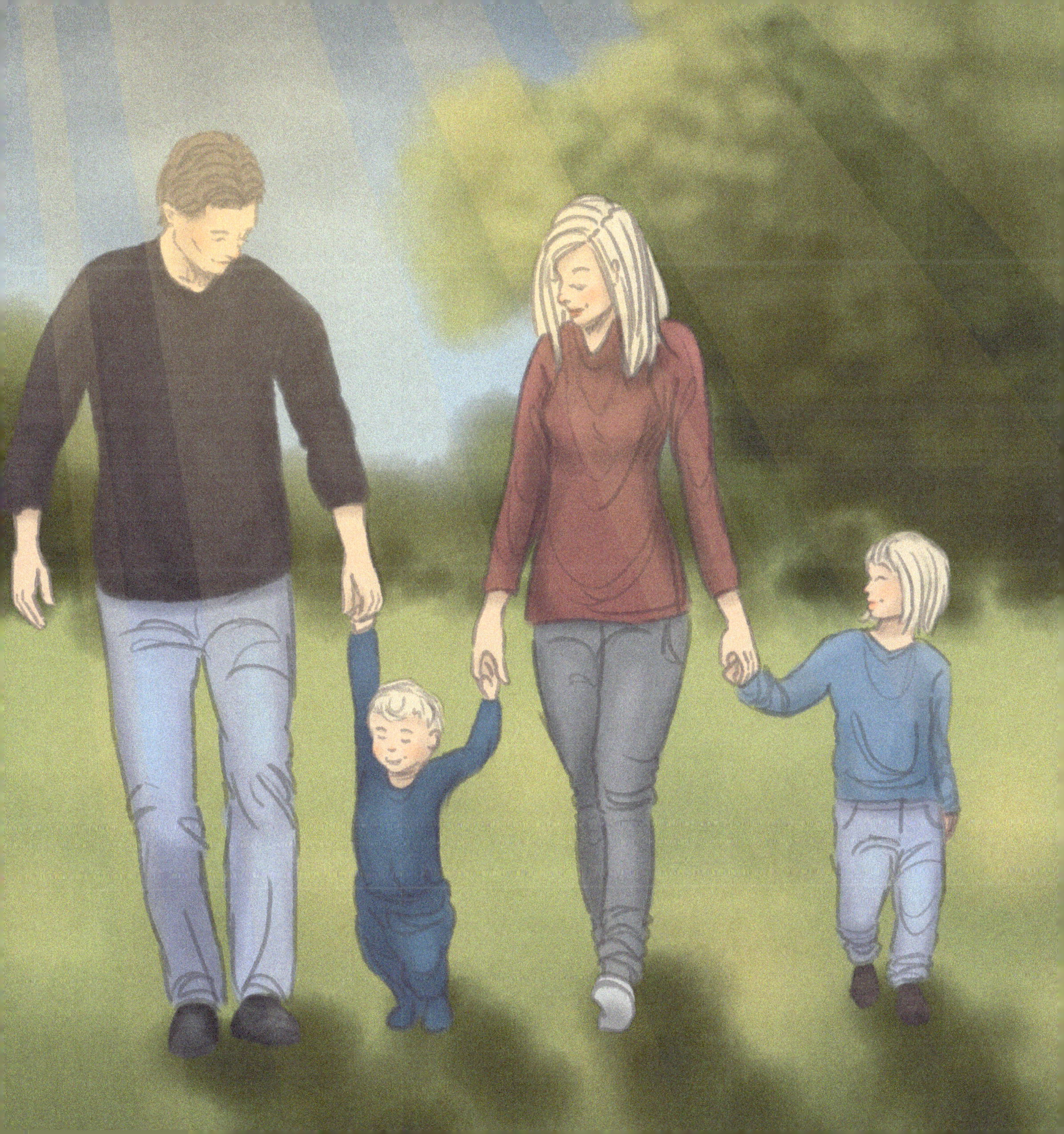

When Daddy was sick, I would make funny faces, and he would laugh. I liked it when he laughed. Mommy and I laughed too.

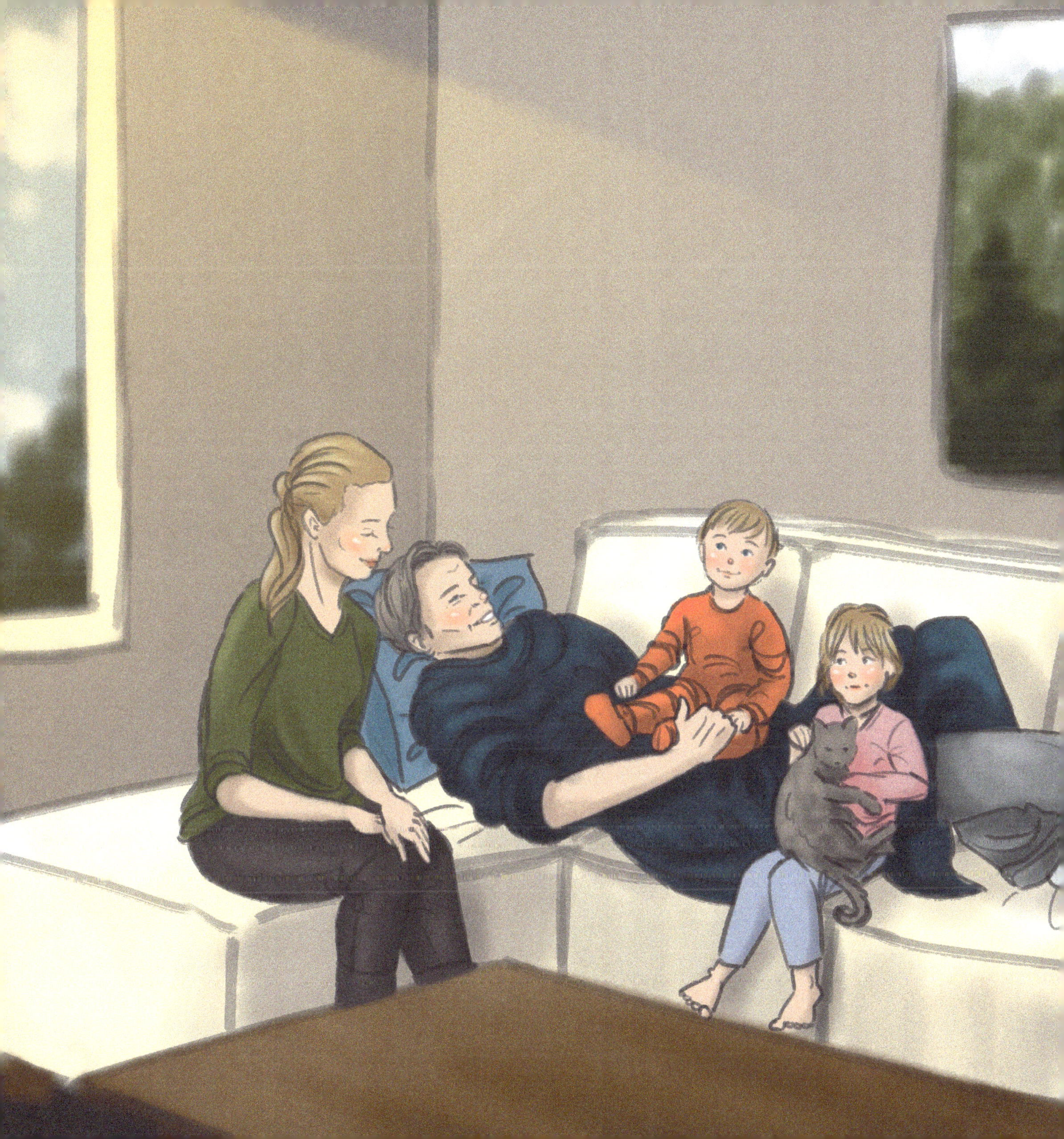

When Daddy died, I didn't want to laugh any more. I cried because I missed him. Mommy picked me up and hugged me. We sat in Daddy's favorite chair together. She said it was okay to be sad. She said sometimes she was sad and also cried. She missed Daddy too.

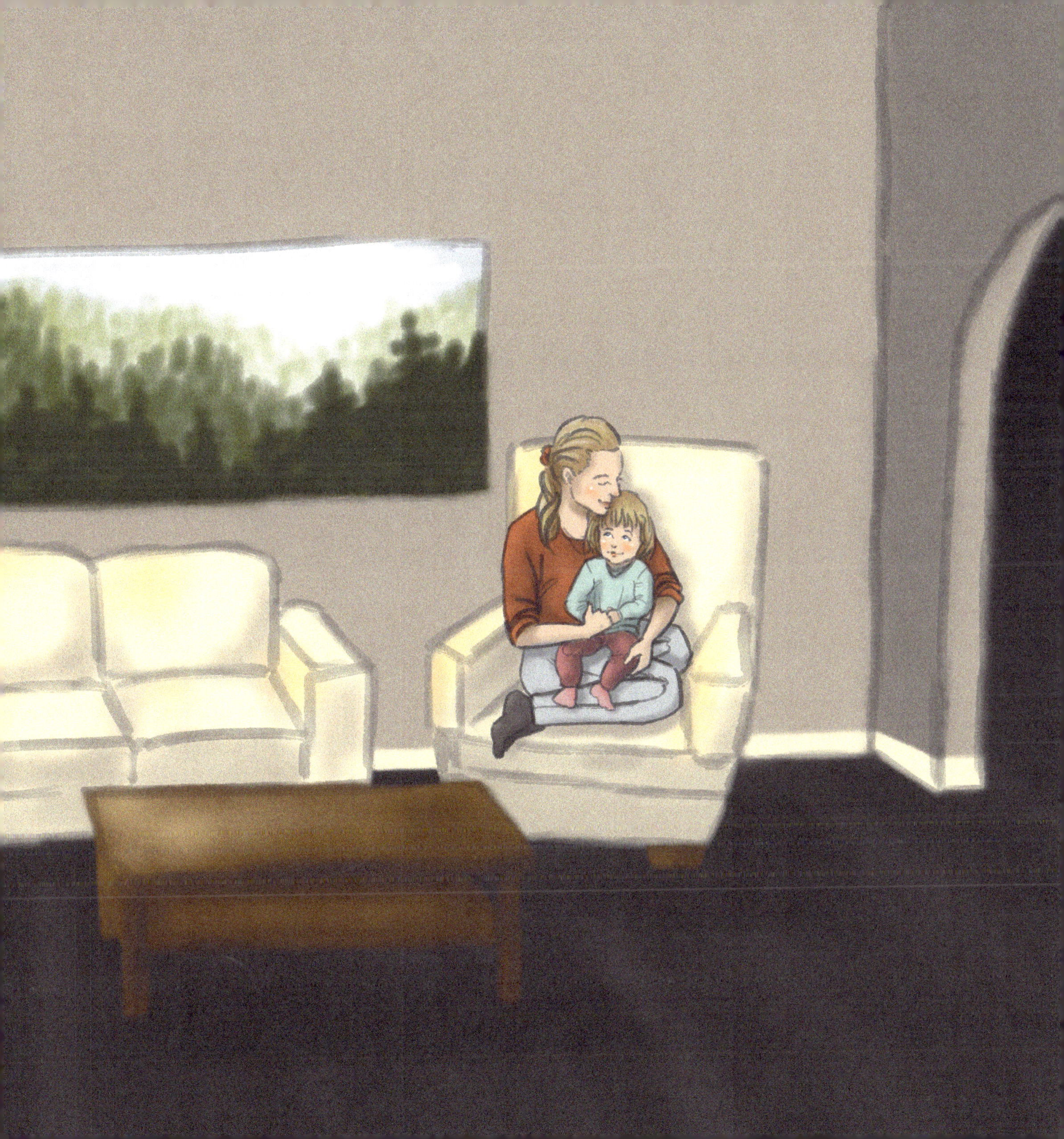

Mommy said Daddy gave me a special gift that would help me keep him close and to remember him. Mommy said that my blue eyes are just like Daddy's. She said that Daddy gave me his blue eyes so that I could see all the things he couldn't see anymore.

He gave me his blue eyes so I could see and remember all the things that made us happy together.

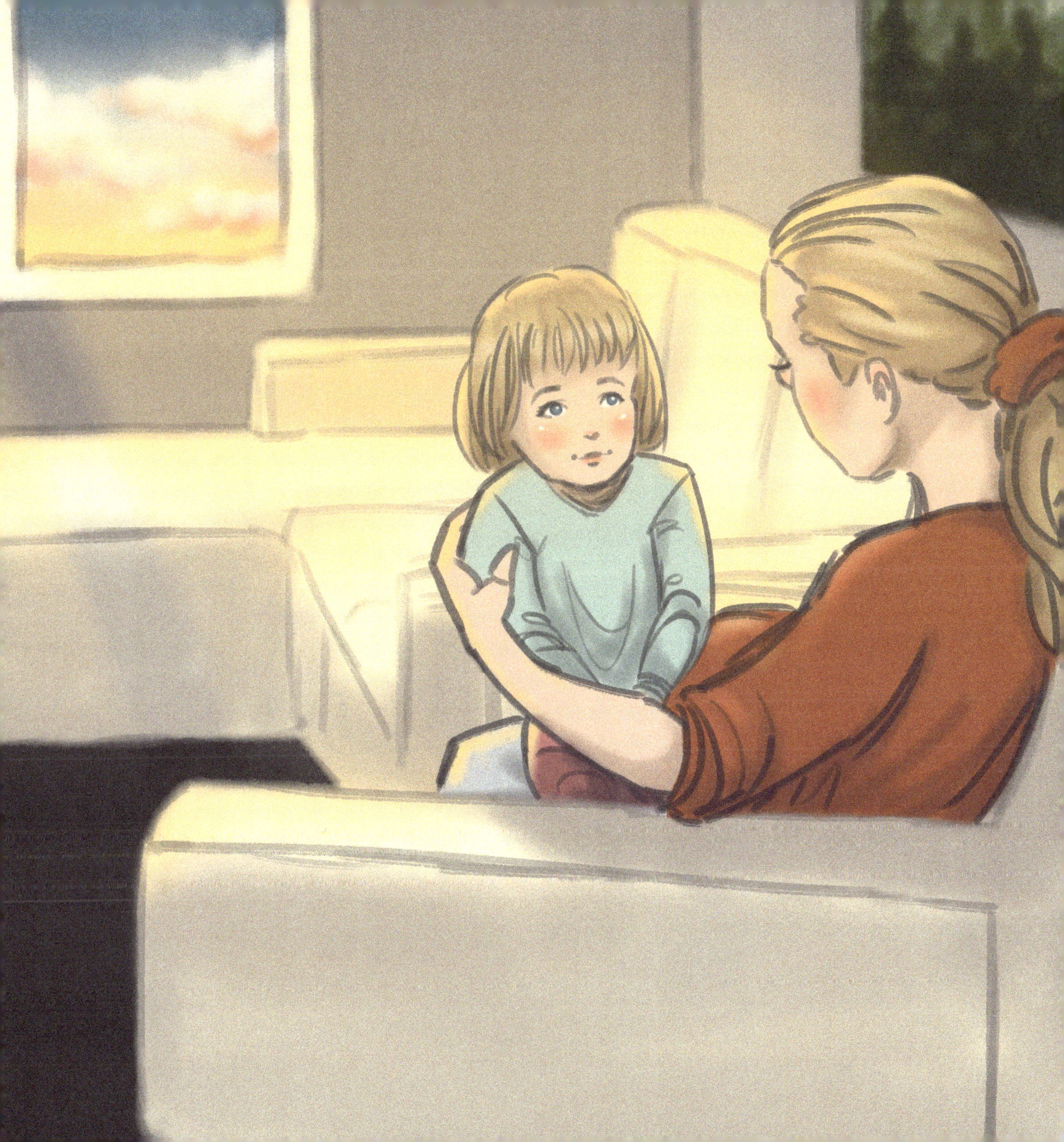

Now when I wake up in the morning, I open my blue eyes and see the sun shining. I remember my daddy's smiling face looking at me.

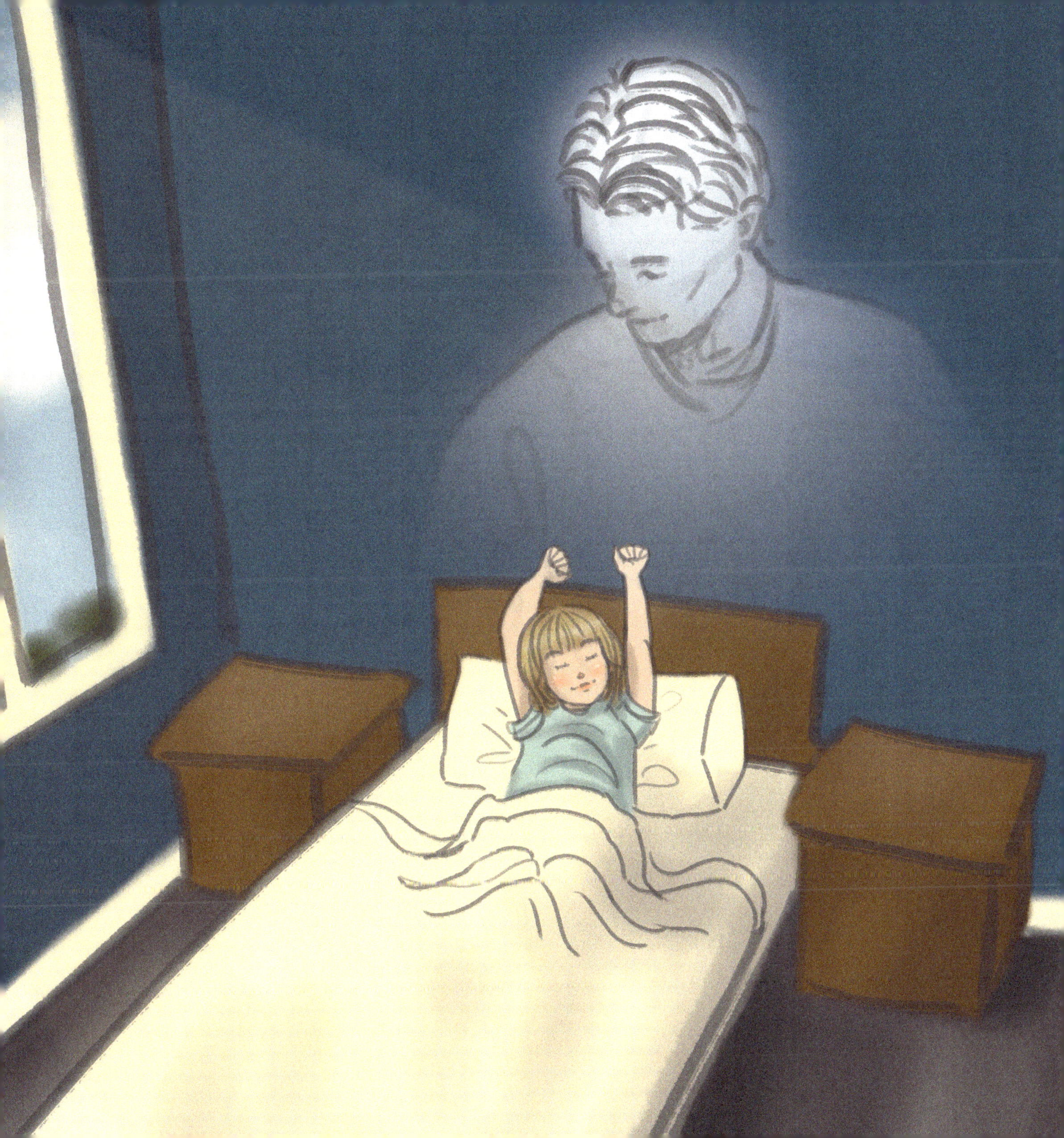

When I watch hockey on TV, I put on Daddy's hockey jersey. I get excited and yell really loud like Daddy did, especially when his favorite team scored a goal.

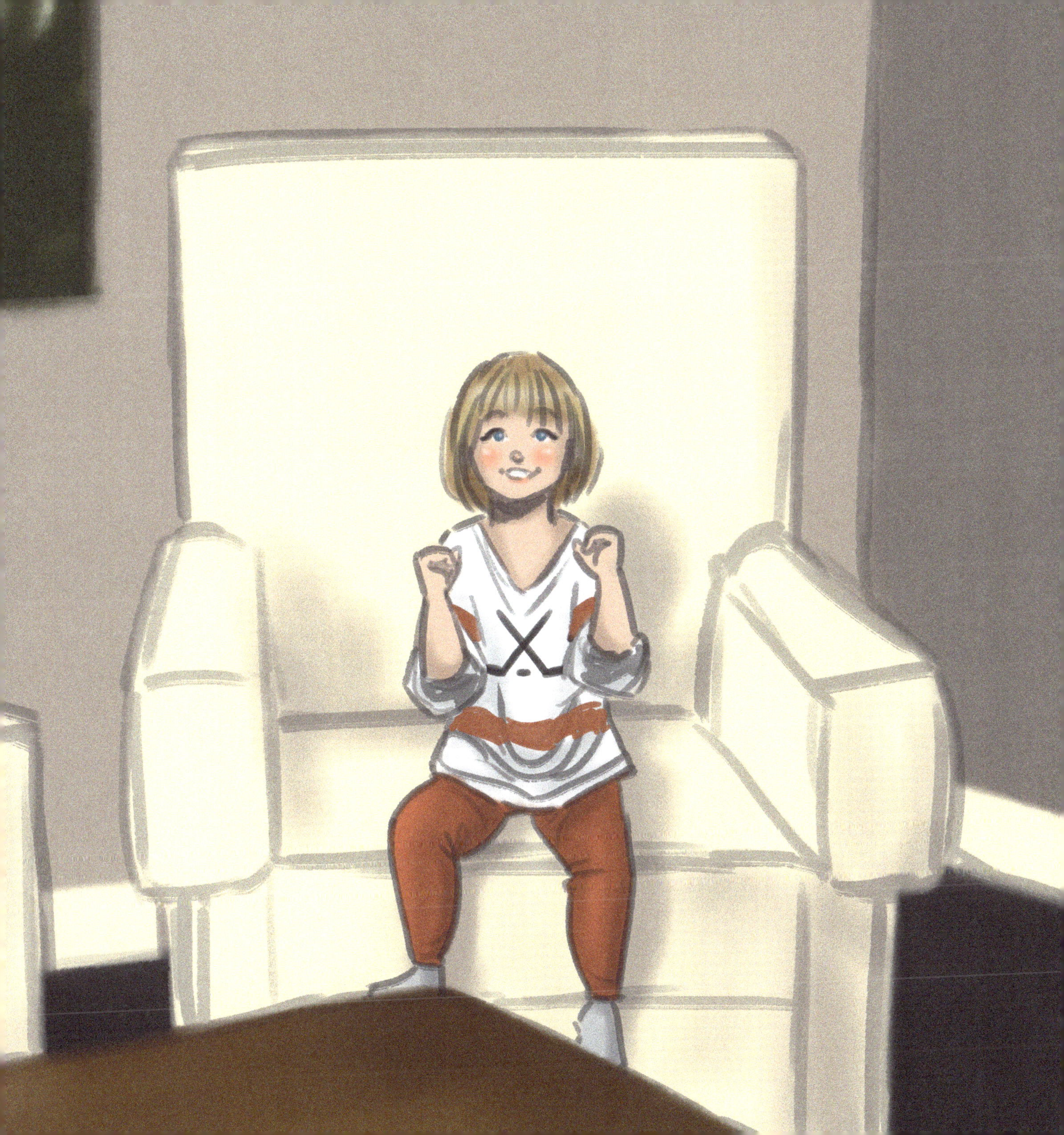

When it snows, I think about Daddy skiing. Now that I am older, I ski too. I come down the hill really fast and know that Daddy's spirit is with me in my heart.

Daddy gave me his blue eyes so I could see the world as he would have shared it with me.

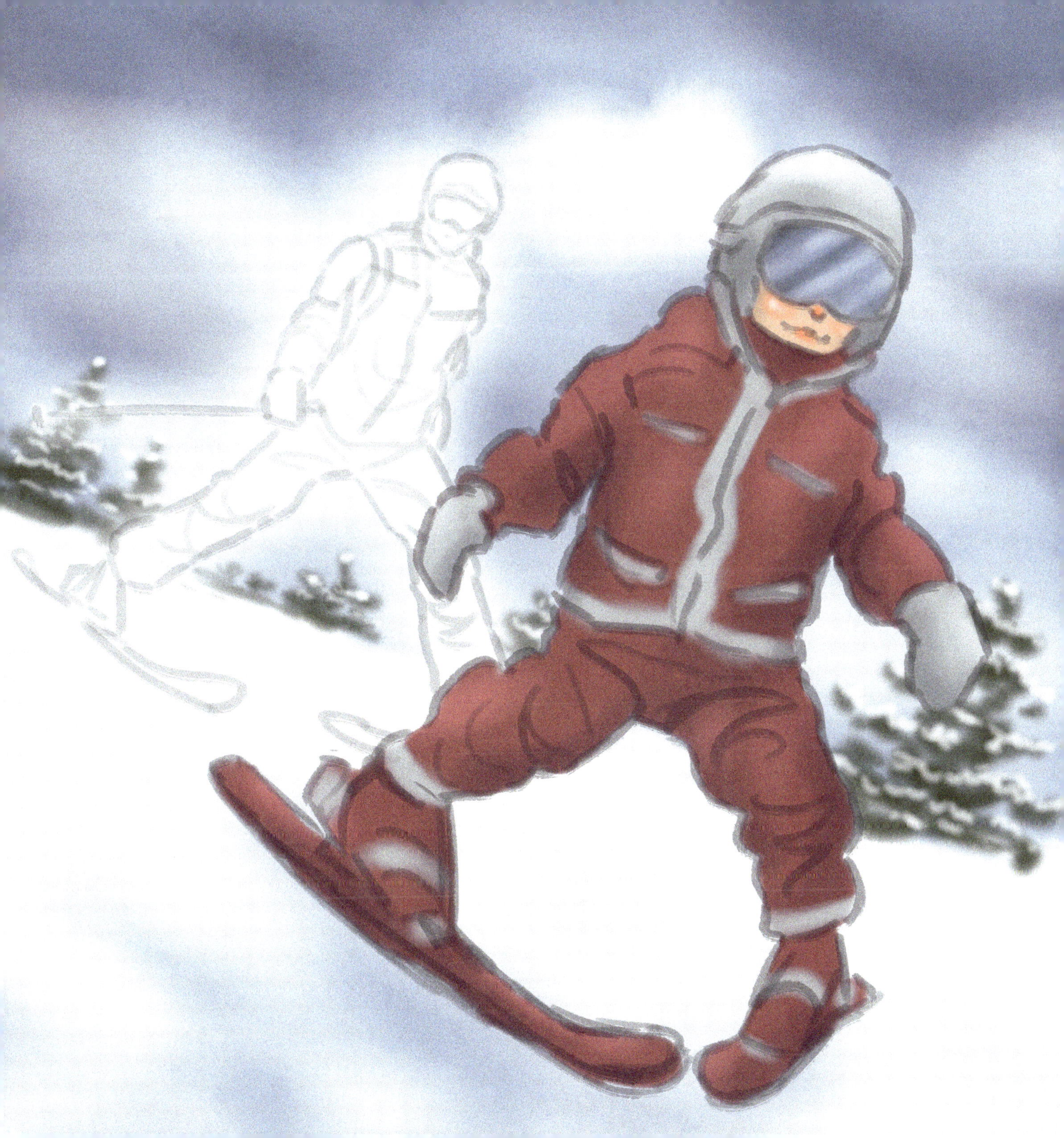

When I go to bed at night, I imagine that my daddy is a police officer angel. I see him looking after all the children on earth.

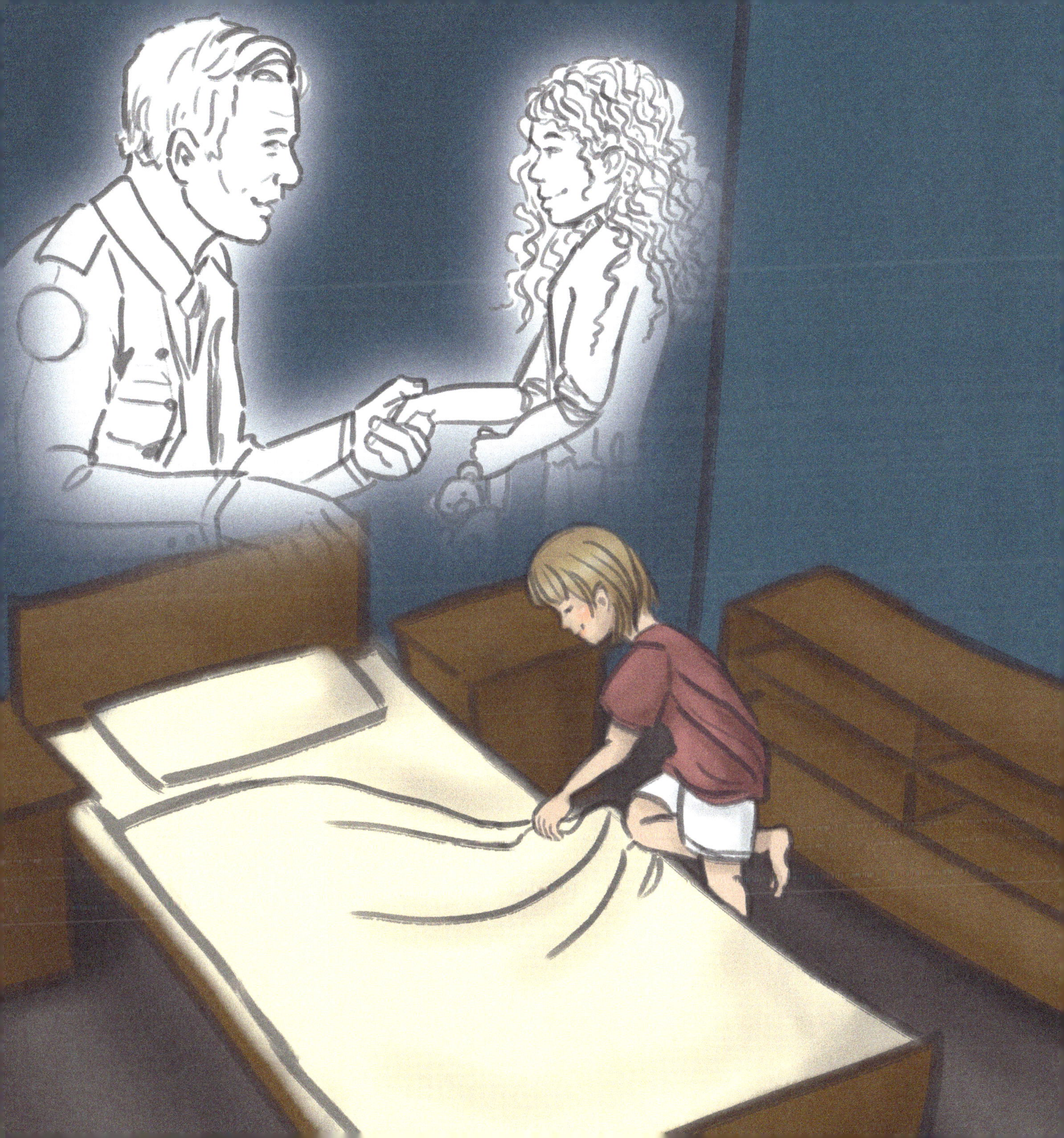

In my dreams, I see Daddy's face, and I see his blue eyes watching me. I imagine him saying, "Be happy little one, I love you, and I am always with you."

I smile, close my eyes and go to sleep.

I love you too, Daddy.

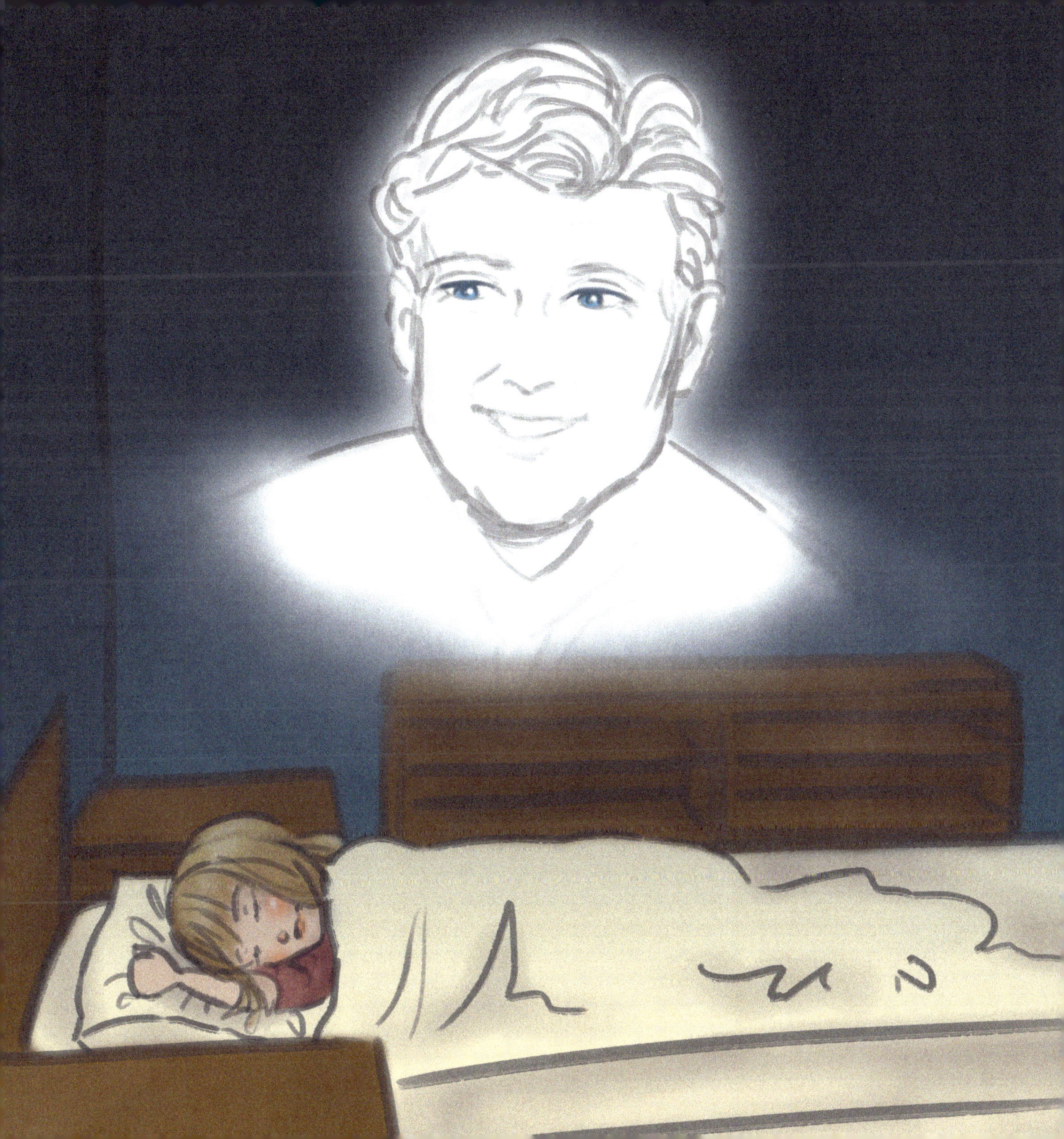

"Carve your name on hearts not tombstones.
A legacy is etched into the minds of others and the stories they share about you."
Shannon Alder

**Dear Parent or Caregiver:**

Talking to children about the death of a loved one isn't easy. Finding the right words to help them understand what happened and why, may be hard for you – especially as you navigate your own feelings of loss and grief. This booklet provides a loving, caring place to come together with your child to share emotions, happy memories and to start the healing process. While the story in this book focuses on the death of a father, the conversations and activities can be modified to reflect the death of any loved one who was close to your child. It's through the sharing of stories and memories that we keep the spirit of our loved ones alive for ourselves and our future generations.

**Things to talk about**

- When you think about your loved one, what do you remember the most?

- What things did you do together? What games did you play? What books did you read? What music did you listen to? What songs did you sing?

- What made you laugh?

- What special things did your loved one teach you?

- The little girl in the story was sad and wanted to cry when she thought about her daddy dying. How do you feel when you think about your loved one dying?

## Things to do

- Make a poster or collage of all the things that remind your child of their loved one. Think about the qualities they share. I have Daddy's blue eyes. I laugh like Grandma. We both liked to ride our bikes.

- Create traditions, unique rituals or remembrance activities to help keep memories alive.

  - Plan a yearly picnic to celebrate your deceased loved one's birthday.

  - Light a candle to honor your loved one during significant holidays.

  - Look through photos of past events and share your stories.

  - Plant a tree in a park where you spent time together.

- Keep something from your child's loved one that has special meaning for your child.

  - Frame a photo and place it in your child's room.

  - Make a memory book together. Fill it with photos, drawings and stories.

  - Create a memory box to store precious items that belonged to your loved one.

- Encourage your child to talk to other family members and friends. Ask them to share their favorite stories about their loved one.

- Create art together. Not all children know how to verbalize their feelings. Some may not be ready or want to. When words fail, drawing and coloring are great ways to express emotions.

## Additional Resources

Websites you can go to for additional information. It's not a complete list, but a good starting point. They represent a variety of ideas and approaches to help you find what will work for you and your child.

- Talking With Kids And Teens About Dying And Death

  - kidsgrief.ca

- How Children Grieve

  - www.todaysparent.com/family/family-life/how-children-grieve/

  - www.socialworktoday.com/archive/030415p20.shtml

- Helping Your Child Deal With Death

  - kidshealth.org/en/parents/death.html

- Helping Kids Cope With Grief

  - www.parents.com/kids/development/behavioral/help-kids-cope-grief/

- Activities For Grieving Children – YouthLight

  - youthlight.com/sample/activities_grieving

CPSIA information can be obtained
at www.ICGtesting.com
Printed in the USA
LVHW071905030219
606243LV00001B/1/P